JOHN PAUL II

JOHN PAUL II

THE POPE FROM POLAND

DEBORAH A. PARKS

A GATEWAY BIOGRAPHY
THE MILLBROOK PRESS
BROOKFIELD, CONNECTICUT

For Catherine Seeberger, who taught me the meaning of
faith, and for my Down Syndrome sister Cathy Keeler,
who taught me the meaning of courage.

Library of Congress Cataloging-in-Publication Data
Parks, Deborah A., 1948-
John Paul II : the Pope from Poland / Deborah Parks.
p. cm. — (A Gateway biography)
Includes index.
Summary: Traces the life of Karol Wojtyla from his childhood and student
years through his ordination as a priest and his life as Pope John Paul II, the
first pope from Poland.
ISBN 0-7613-2320-1 (lib. bdg.)
1. John Paul II, Pope, 1920—Juvenile literature. 2. Popes—Biography—
Juvenile literature. [1. John Paul II, Pope, 1920– 2. Popes.]
I. Title. II. Series.
BX1378.5 .P3695 2002 282'.092—dc21
[B] 2001045026

Cover photograph courtesy of AP/Wide World Photos

Photographs courtesy of AP/Wide World Photos: pp. 2, 9, 26, 33, 41; Gamma
Presse: pp. 6 (© Anticoli/Vandeville), 10 (© F. Lochon); Gamma Presse
© Archives Jean-Paul II: pp. 14, 15, 16, 25, 29, 30; SIPA Press: p. 12
(© Laski); National Archives: p. 20 (#NWDNS-SFF-SSF-52); © Rudi
Frey/TimePix: p. 39 (both); © Reuters NewMedia Inc./Corbis: p. 43; Archive
Photos: p. 45 (© Paolo Cocco)

Published by The Millbrook Press, Inc.
2 Old New Milford Road
Brookfield, Connecticut 06804
www.millbrookpress.com

Contents

St. Peter's Square— where many church celebrations are held

A New Kind of Pope

Nobody knew what to expect as the sun set on Rome, Italy, on October 16, 1978. In St. Peter's Square, thousands of people stared at a small chimney on the Sistine Chapel. Everybody waited to see a puff of smoke. A white puff would mean that officials for the Roman Catholic Church had elected a new pope. A black puff meant the church officials had not yet agreed on who should lead the church. So far only black puffs had appeared.

Inside the chapel, church officials voted for the eighth time. When the results were read, Karol Wojtyla slumped forward in his chair and cried. As a schoolboy growing up in Poland, Wojtyla had once said he had no interest in becoming a priest. Now church officials had elected him pope—the church's highest office. Would he accept the offer?

There was a long pause before Wojtyla raised his head. He then replied, "It is God's will. I accept."

As a white puff of smoke curled from the chapel's chimney, the crowd in St. Peter's Square went wild. They knew the world had a new pope! But who was he?

At 6:45 P.M. a church official made the announcement. He called out the name—Karol Wojtyla. It sounded something like *Voy-tih-whu*.

The name shocked the crowd into silence. For 456 years, officials for the Roman Catholic Church had picked Italian popes. But this was not an Italian name. A voice in the crowd yelled out, "a foreign pope!"

As the minutes passed, people grew restless waiting to see what this foreign pope was like. Finally, the new fifty-eight-year-old pope walked onto the balcony. Dressed in long white robes and standing nearly 6 feet (183 centimeters) tall, he looked young and fit. He flashed a broad smile at the crowd.

Everybody expected Wojtyla to follow tradition. He would, they thought, deliver a blessing in Latin—the official language of the church. Instead the new pope stunned the crowd by speaking in Italian. "Even if I am not sure I can

Karol Wojtyla greets the crowd in St. Peter's Square after being named pope in 1978.

express myself in your—I mean *our*—Italian language," he began, "you will correct me if I make a mistake."

The crowd laughed and applauded wildly. This pope might be foreign, but he spoke perfect Italian.

The inauguration of Pope John Paul II in 1978

Meanwhile, in another part of Rome, a dentist turned up his radio so he could hear the new pope speak. "What kind of accent is that?" he asked his patient.

"Polish!" replied his patient, Jerzy Kluger. "It's Wojtyla," he yelled excitedly. "I know him!"

"You know the pope?" asked the doubtful dentist.

"He is my friend!" explained Kluger. "He is like me, a boy from Wadowice, Poland!"

Every person who becomes pope picks a new name. Wojtyla chose the name of John Paul II. But Kluger explained that in Wadowice people called him "Lolek," the nickname given to him by his mother.

A few days later the new pope was inaugurated in Rome. Catholics from around the world came to honor him.

CHILD OF POLAND

Karol "Lolek" Wojtyla was born on May 18, 1920, in Wadowice. The town lies in the foothills of the Beskidy Mountains in southern Poland. In the 1920s about 6,000 Roman Catholics and 1,500 Jews lived in the town.

Lolek's father, Karol Sr., was an army clerk. His mother, Emilia, was a former schoolteacher. She worked part-time as a seamstress, mending people's clothes.

Along with his parents, Lolek shared a three-room apartment with his older brother, Edmund. "Mundek," as the family called him, left for medical college when Lolek was four.

Lolek's mother, father, and brother, Mundek

From the time he was born, Lolek's mother wanted him to be a priest. She showed him how to make the sign of the cross when he prayed. She taught him to read the Bible. When he was old enough, she sent Lolek scrambling down the stairs to the sandstone Catholic church across the street. Every day, for his whole childhood, little Lolek went to mass, or religious services, at the church. "My Lolek will become a great person," Emilia boasted.

Neighbors shook their heads at this idea. Lolek seemed like most other children in Wadowice. Although he received top grades, he was no bookworm. At recess he tumbled into the cobblestone town square to play with the other boys. One of his earliest playmates was Jerzy Kluger, who was nicknamed "Jurek."

The two boys learned to play soccer on the streets. Because the church was close to the square, the soccer ball sometimes slammed into the church wall. More than one black-robed priest warned the future pope to play elsewhere. Eventually, Lolek played for a school team made up mostly of Jewish boys. Visitors to Wadowice today can still see the field where "Lolek the Goalie" played soccer.

Sad Times

Lolek knew from an early age that his mother was not well. She sometimes fainted or cried out in pain. At such times, she would beg her husband, "Please don't leave me alone." On April 13, 1929, Emilia cried out for the last time. As Lolek headed home from third grade, his teacher

The young Lolek

caught up with him. "Your mother has died," she told him.

The eight year old surprised his teacher by replying, "It is God's will." Lolek didn't cry. Ten years later, he finally poured out his grief in a poem about his mother's death. "So many years without you," he mourned.

After Emilia died, Karol Sr. tried to be both father and mother to Lolek. Because he had retired from the army to care for his wife, money was scarce. But Karol Sr. came up with ideas to make his son's life happier. He ripped apart his old army uniforms and made them into clothes for Lolek. He took Lolek to the hills, mountains, and rivers for sports and picnics. He

Lolek (bottom row on right) and his
father (in overcoat) on a school trip with Lolek's
classmates and teachers

turned the parlor into an indoor soccer field and played soccer with him.

Slowly life got better for Lolek. At age ten he began high school, which has eight grades in Poland. He became an altar boy, and helped the priest during mass. After school, Lolek and Jurek usually did homework together at

Lolek at age twelve in Wadowice

Lolek's house. Karol Sr. quizzed the boys on dates in Polish history and taught them about Polish writers and artists. Lolek visited the Klugers, too. Sometimes Lolek and Jurek sat glued to the radio listening to soccer games.

But of all the things he did, Lolek liked being with his older brother, Mundek, best of all. On breaks from medical school, Mundek, who was a college soccer star, often challenged Lolek to dribbling matches in the streets or took him swimming, hiking, or skiing.

Mundek also encouraged his little brother's love of the theater. Lolek's neighbors, the Kotlarczyks, used their home to perform plays and welcomed Lolek to join them. Lolek discovered that he had a talent for singing and dancing. When Mundek became a doctor, he invited Lolek to perform for his patients.

Lolek adored his brother. But when he was twelve, a terrible thing happened. Mundek caught scarlet fever—a deadly disease—and died. After that, recalled Lolek, "I became a motherless only child."

TEEN YEARS

Lolek found comfort in the daily schedule set by his father. Karol Sr. set times for meals, school, play, homework, exercise, and church. He had Lolek study in a chilly room to toughen him and teach him to concentrate. Looking back on his childhood, Lolek said his father's teachings prepared him for the life of a priest.

Karol Sr. would have smiled at this compliment. He truly wanted Lolek to become a priest. "I would like to be certain before I die that you will commit yourself to God's service," he once wished. But the priesthood would come later.

At age fourteen, Lolek had other ideas. He wanted to be an actor, and his father never discouraged him. Soon Lolek became the star of a theater group made up of students. Not only did he sing, but the future pope also took dancing lessons.

Now Lolek's circle of friends included both girls and boys. He formed close friendships with student actresses, Halina Krolikiewicz and Ginka Beer. Ginka, the Jewish next-door neighbor, practiced reading parts with Lolek. "I know you have a girl," worried his father. However, Lolek never dated. As Lolek put it, he had one passion—"the theater."

As graduation neared, an important church official paid a visit to Lolek's high school. Lolek, the best speaker in the school, was picked to welcome him. He startled the official by speaking in perfect Latin. The official turned to Lolek's teacher and asked, "What will he do after graduation? Will he attend the seminary [school for priests]?"

Lolek spoke for himself. No, he would not enter the seminary. "I plan to take Polish literature," he announced.

The official sighed, "Too bad, too bad!"

Lolek graduated at the top of his high-school class. The year was 1938—a terrible time in world history. A dictator in Germany named Adolf Hitler had risen to power. Hitler talked of building a new empire in Europe.

Ginka Beer's family was alarmed. That summer, they told Karol Sr. that they were leaving Poland. They feared that Poland might follow in the footsteps of Germany. There, supporters of Adolf Hitler, known as Nazis, wanted to kill all Jews.

Karol Sr. tried to talk the family into staying. "All Poles are not anti-Semitic [haters of Jews]," he said. "You know I am not." But the family insisted. They would go to Palestine. The British, who ruled Palestine at the time, had promised the Jews a homeland. Later it was named Israel.

Ginka made a prediction: "Have you seen what's going on with the Jews in Germany? Well, it's going to happen here!"

A short time after Ginka and her family left, Lolek bade farewell to Jurek, who headed off to college in Warsaw, Poland's capital. Lolek then set out for college in Krakow. Karol Sr. joined him, arranging for them to live in the home of a relative.

NAZI INVASION

Lolek slipped easily into his new life. He adopted what the Poles called "the poetic look." He let his hair grow long. He wore rough cotton pants, a wrinkled black jacket, and no necktie. He took a heavy load of classes, but found time to write poetry, study French, and join an acting group.

The one activity that Lolek avoided was fighting. "He's not a coward," Jurek Kluger explained. "He just doesn't get into quarrels." By 1939, however, it was hard for Lolek to stay out of fights. Anti-Semitism, as Ginka had warned, was spreading. Attacks on Jews had forced Jurek to leave college. Meanwhile, Lolek stood up for Jewish students at his school.

Nazi troops parade through Warsaw, Poland.

Then there was the question of Germany. Hitler had demanded land from Poland, but Poland refused to give in to his bullying. Lolek was caught in the middle. As a student, he was not required to serve actively in the military. However, if war came, no one could escape the fighting—not even Lolek the peacemaker.

On the morning of September 1, 1939, Lolek attended mass at Wawel Cathedral. As he prayed, German airplanes swooped down on the military barracks just a few blocks away. Pilots fired guns on people in the streets. Then they dropped bombs.

Screaming sirens and bomb blasts sent people fleeing for safety. Lolek found himself alone with his old religion teacher from Wadowice—Father Figlewicz. As bombs shook Krakow, the priest asked the former altar boy to serve mass. "We have to celebrate mass, in spite of everything," he said. "Pray God to spare Poland!"

As soon as the two-person mass ended, Lolek cried, "I've got to go. My father's at home alone." When Lolek reached the apartment, he and his father decided to leave the city.

While German troops poured in from the west, the Wojtylas joined people fleeing eastward on foot. About 100 miles (160 kilometers) into their flight, they ran into Soviet troops. Germany and the Soviet Union had struck a secret deal. They promised not to attack each other and to divide up Poland between them.

With no place to go, Lolek and Karol Sr. returned to Krakow. Within two weeks, Poland ceased to exist as an independent nation. Great Britain, which had signed a treaty promising to defend Poland, declared war on Germany. But it was too late to save Poland from the horrors soon to follow. World War II had begun.

WORLD WAR II

The war robbed Lolek of his youth. The Nazis declared total war on the Polish people and their culture. They shut down universities, closed schools, and took over churches.

Each day Lolek saw people arrested, beaten, or shot to death in the streets. The Nazis seized his professors, then local priests and nuns. Many of them were shipped to concentration camps—prisons that meant death for most people. One camp, Auschwitz, lay just outside of Lolek's hometown of Wadowice.

On October 26, 1939, the Nazis ordered all Poles between the ages of fourteen and sixty to work for them. They forced Jews over the age of twelve to do the same. The Nazis then cut off the pension of Karol Sr., who was now more than sixty years old. Nineteen-year-old Lolek desperately needed a job. Friends helped by finding him work at a stone quarry.

For eight hours a day, Lolek smashed rocks with a pickax and dragged the rubble to a railroad car. He worked in weather so cold that he had to coat his face with petroleum jelly to keep it from freezing. The job paid barely enough money to buy potatoes, bread, and an occasional cabbage for him and his father.

Under the crush of work and poverty, Lolek's face grew thin and bony. He hunched over when he walked. Yet he refused to give up the things he loved: Poland, the theater, and, most of all, the church.

Despite the threat of death, Lolek joined an underground, or secret, theater group. He and his friends performed Polish plays and read poetry in people's apartments. Some of the works were written by Lolek.

Lolek also disobeyed the Nazis in another way. Hitler had demanded that priests preach only "what we want them to preach." But Polish priests refused to obey. They got lay people, non-priests, to help keep religion alive by working secretly with young people. One lay teacher, Jan Leopold Tyranowski, asked Lolek to join him.

Tyranowski influenced Lolek deeply. He taught Lolek that through deep and silent prayer a person could get close to God. And with this closeness, a person could endure all suffering.

Tyranowski's message came at a turning point in Lolek's life. On February 18, 1941, Lolek returned home to find his father dead. The future pope now felt truly alone—an orphan. Years later he would write, "At twenty I had already lost all the people I loved."

After the death of Karol Sr., the Nazis increased their efforts to rid Poland of all Jews and people who opposed Germany in any way. Lolek prayed more deeply than ever before. He felt unsure of his acting career. Did he have another calling, or purpose, in life? By the fall of 1942, Lolek had found an answer. He shared it with Father Figlewicz. "I want to be a priest," he declared.

Father Figlewicz arranged for Lolek to see Archbishop Adam Sapieha. He was the same church official whom Lolek had welcomed to his high school in Wadowice. Although the Nazis forbade the training of new priests, Sapieha had just opened an underground seminary. Lolek was among the first ten students.

Lolek now led two lives. By day he worked as a laborer. By night he studied to be a priest.

In August 1944, the Nazis swept through the city in a search for "resisters." They arrested more than eight thousand men and young boys. Lolek escaped the roundup, or massive arrest, but Archbishop Sapieha decided it was time to hide Lolek and other students at his home until the end of the war.

For Krakow, the end came early in 1945. Mad with power, Hitler had attacked the Soviet Union. The action drove the Soviet Union to join with the nations fighting Germany. After the Soviets forced the Germans to retreat, they pushed eastward and "freed" Poland. Now Poland fell under Soviet control. On January 19, Soviet tanks entered Krakow.

THE YOUNG PRIEST

With the war over, Lolek emerged from his secret seminary. He returned to college and got his degree. On November 1, 1946, Sapieha personally ordained, or appointed, him a priest.

The young priest, Father Wojtyla

On November 2, Father Wojtyla, as Lolek was now known, performed his first mass. He chose the Wawel Cathedral—the place where he had been on the day of the Nazi invasion. As Wojtyla explained, he wanted to show his belief in Polish freedom.

But Wojtyla did not stay in Poland for long. Sapieha had special plans for him. On November 15, he sent Wojtyla and another talented young priest to Rome. Sapieha told them to earn higher degrees in religion.

Wojtyla (top row, right) at Belgian College in Rome, Italy

Two years later, in June 1948, Wojtyla returned home with his second degree. One of his first tasks was to attend a high-school reunion in Wadowice.

As Lolek sat at his old desk, only about half of the class of 1938 answered "present" to the roll call. Seeing all the empty desks reminded him of what the war had cost. Almost every Polish family had lost someone. Six million Poles had died or had been killed. Half were Jews. Only about 50,000 Jews remained in all of Poland.

Wojtyla wanted to know what had happened to the Klugers. From a classmate he found out that Jurek and his father were shipped to Russia to fight on the battlefront, but the rest of the family had been killed at Auschwitz.

Wojtyla couldn't understand why his life had been spared. To seek an answer to this question, Wojtyla asked to enter a monastery so he could spend his life in prayer. Sapieha refused—not once but four times. When another official asked the reason, Sapieha replied: "With the war over, we have only a few priests, and Wojtyla is badly needed."

By this time, Sapieha—along with the rest of the world—knew that the Soviet Union planned to keep Poland. Instead of pulling out its troops at the end of the war, the Soviets announced that Poland would now be part of the Soviet Union. The Soviet Union set up a Polish government based on communism—a system in which the government controls every aspect of life.

The Soviets banned all religion inside their borders. But they stopped short of closing churches in Poland. Still, the Soviets made no secret of their intention to limit church activities.

Sapieha believed that Polish Roman Catholics were in great danger. In 1948 he decided to see if Wojtyla could handle the job of protecting them. Sapieha sent his twenty-eight-year-old priest to Niegowic, a rural village without electricity, running water, or a sewage system. His job was to help a local priest spread the Roman Catholic religion.

When Wojtyla arrived, villagers saw a skinny young man with glasses and a beat-up suitcase. But Wojtyla proved more fit than villagers first imagined. He rose mornings at 5 A.M., said mass, taught religion at five elementary schools, and visited villages that had not seen a priest in years. He helped people dig ditches and worked alongside them in the fields. He took young people on hikes and played soccer or volleyball with them. He spent evenings organizing plays or singing popular songs around a bonfire.

However, the prying eyes of Communists were everywhere. The local secret police hired a spy to inform on Wojtyla. But Wojtyla continued his work.

After seven months, Sapieha sent Wojtyla to his next assignment—in the bustling city of Krakow. Wojtyla again adapted quickly. He not only held mass at a big church there, but he also taught at the university. And he

Wojtyla enjoyed bicycling and other sports most of his life.

wasted no time in taking young people on camping trips. The fact that the Communists forbade priests from leading youth groups outside the church made the trips even more exciting.

As in Niegowic, Communist spies reported on Wojtyla's every move. Sapieha sensed the danger. Just before he died in the summer of 1951, he instructed Archbishop Eugeniusz Baziak to protect Wojtyla. In late 1951, Baziak told Wojtyla to take a two-year leave of absence. Go back to school, said Baziak. That decision saved Wojtyla from going to jail.

Wojtyla becomes bishop of Krakow, 1958.

ADVANCEMENT

After Wojtyla completed his studies, he went on to teach college and write books. He also held counseling sessions on marriage. To the Communists, he looked more like a scholar than a troublemaker. So they shrugged their shoulders when Baziak appointed him bishop of Krakow in 1958.

In keeping with tradition, the church gave the new bishop some gifts of his choosing. Wojtyla asked for a canoe, a new tent, and a portable desk to take on camping trips. But Wojtyla had less and less time to escape to the mountains. He was now too much in the public spotlight.

As bishop, Wojtyla came face-to-face with the Communists. He had to figure out ways to protect the church. Sometimes that meant standing up to the government. When officials refused to give Wojtyla a permit to build a church, for example, he held masses on the building site. He showed up day after day, in all kinds of weather, until the officials gave in.

Wojtyla's actions also got the attention of church officials at the Vatican. Located in Rome, the Vatican is the center of government for the Roman Catholic Church. Between 1962 and 1965, Wojtyla attended important meetings at the Vatican in which changes in church policy were discussed.

Wojtyla dazzled church leaders from around the world with his energy and speaking talents. He supported new ideas. He said it was important for the church to defend the human rights of all people, not just Roman Catholics. He argued in favor of religious freedom and unity among all Christians. He told church leaders that it was a good

VATICAN CITY

The pope is not only the head of the Roman Catholic Church, but of an entire nation known as Vatican City, or the Holy See. Located in the heart of Rome, Vatican City is the smallest independent nation in the world. It covers just 0.17 square mile (0.44 sq km) and has about 850 full-time residents. Vatican City has its own flag and establishes relations with other nations. Its one national holiday is Installation of the Pope Day.

idea to hold masses in the everyday language of the people, instead of Latin, and to involve worshipers in church policy.

The one thing Wojtyla refused to do at these meetings was to attack communism. He had made it a policy to compromise with the Communists, when possible. He stood up to them in matters of religion, but did not openly criticize the government. "I'm not very interested in politics," he repeatedly said.

The tactic was a good one. In late 1963, when it came time to appoint a new archbishop of Krakow, the Communists picked Wojtyla. In 1967 they allowed the Vatican to name Wojtyla as one of two Polish cardinals.

Wojtyla gets a warm Polish welcome when he returns from Rome after being appointed cardinal.

The secret police now issued a report on Wojtyla to the government. The report noted: "It seems politics is not his strong suit. . . . He lacks organizing and leadership qualities." Wojtyla would soon prove them wrong.

SPEAKING OUT

Starting in 1968, the government saw a new Wojtyla.

That spring, the Communists canceled a patriotic play in Warsaw. Instead of remaining quiet, students marched through the streets shouting slogans against the Soviets. The police beat and arrested the marchers. Then the government shut down universities. Risking an attack on the church, Wojtyla defended the students.

Next, in December 1970, workers marched through the streets when the government increased food prices. They demanded higher wages and a return to old prices. This time the government ordered tanks to fire on workers. The violence shook Wojtyla.

In a New Year's Eve sermon, Wojtyla did what the Soviets feared the most. He spoke out against the government, calling for the "right to bread, the right to freedom, [and] . . . liberty."

Wojtyla now began to work side by side with the underground groups backed by Poland's other cardinal, Stefan Wysznski. He helped smuggle Bibles into neighboring nations where the Soviets banned the practice of religion. He also ordained priests to serve in secret churches in these same nations.

OFFICIALS OF THE
ROMAN CATHOLIC CHURCH

Imagine a triangle, and you will have a fairly good idea of
how the Roman Catholic Church is organized. At the top of
the triangle is the pope, the head of the church. Next come
the cardinals, who act as the pope's advisers. Together the
cardinals, who are appointed by the various popes, form the
College of Cardinals. The college elects the pope.

Below the cardinals are the archbishops. The archbishops rule over an area called an archdiocese. They make
sure church rules are followed and supervise the work of
bishops, who manage areas called dioceses. Each diocese is
divided into a number of parishes, each of which is run by a
priest. The priests, who form the base of the triangle, do the
day-to-day work of the church.

In 1976 and 1977, workers and police clashed during
protest marches in cities throughout Poland. The time had
come, believed Wojtyla, to win greater freedom for his
homeland and the church. The Polish people, united by the
church, were ready to stand together. "The only way for
peace and national unity," he told thousands of young peo-

ple at a youth rally in late 1977, "is through . . . respect for the rights of man, for the rights of citizens and Poles."

Wojtyla worried about Soviet power. He had seen Soviet troops and tanks move into other Communist-ruled nations that called for freedom. No country tried to stop the bloodshed. He wondered if anybody would help Poland. What Wojtyla could not guess was that he himself would soon be given the power to help Poland. On September 28, 1978, he received word that the pope had died in his sleep. Within weeks, he found himself at the head of the Roman Catholic Church. Now he would be listened to by people around the world.

The news that Wojtyla had been elected pope stunned the Soviets, but the Polish people celebrated. Crowds poured into the streets, holding candles and waving Polish flags. Bells rang in churches everywhere.

Some three thousand Poles set out for the Vatican. They went to support *their* pope on the day of his inauguration.

THE NEW POPE

From day one, the pope set a pace that exhausted his aides. After the inauguration, he held a mass, visited a bishop in the hospital, and then hosted a party for his

THE POPE'S DAY

When not traveling, the pope follows a simple routine. He rises at 5 A.M., and by 6:15 he is dressed and praying in his private chapel. At 7 A.M., the pope celebrates mass in his chapel. The mass used to be closed to the public, but Pope John Paul II invites up to forty people to join him, often asking them to breakfast as well. After breakfast, between 9 A.M. and 11 A.M., the pope writes or dictates letters and reads news summaries gathered for him by his staff.

The pope spends the rest of his day holding both public and private meetings with visitors from all over the world. After lunch he usually has a brief nap. He has dinner around 5 P.M.

The pope tries to set aside a part of each day for some kind of exercise, such as an evening walk. Typically he goes to bed between 11 P.M. and midnight, but sometimes he reads late into the night.

Polish friends in Rome, including his old friend Jerzy. Thereafter, the pope rarely ate alone. He shared his meals with everyone from world leaders, to old friends, to factory workers, to the homeless. Usually he served some of his favorite foods from Poland.

In his first hundred days, Pope John Paul II showed the path he would follow in the years ahead. He spoke out against violence, war, and the death penalty. He called for an end to religious hatred. He called for human rights and freedom of religion.

When it came to the church, the pope firmly upheld traditional teachings. He believed that priests and nuns should devote their lives to the service of God. So he reminded them of their vows of celibacy—a promise not to marry or have children. He accepted that men and women played different roles within the church. So he rejected the idea of women priests. He believed marriages and children were sacred, or blessed. So he spoke out against divorce and new methods of family planning.

Some reformers thought the pope was being old-fashioned. But he refused to bend. The church had been the one thing he could depend on in life. He would not change its most basic beliefs now.

The pope took his message to all corners of the earth. In the next twenty-five years, he would travel more than a half million miles and visit more than 120 countries. On a visit to Africa in 1980 the pope declared: "I speak in the name of those who have no voice."

The pope visits Ghana during his 1980 trip to Africa (top). In a 1987 trip to Poland, he visits a concentration camp (bottom).

As Communist officials feared, the pope included the Poles among the "voiceless" people of the world. In 1979 he planned a tour of Poland. The Soviets wanted to block the visit, believing that it would lead to even more anti-Communist protests there. But the world was watching, so they gave in.

On June 2, a plane carrying the pope landed in Warsaw. The pope had made it a practice to kneel and kiss the ground of every country he visited. It was his way of blessing the people who lived there. When he kissed the Polish soil, the Poles went wild.

As he left Poland ten days later, the pope fought back tears. He told a journalist: "I hope, I hope, I hope to meet you again in this country, I hope. . . ."

A CLOSE CALL

Bullets nearly robbed the pope of his dream. On May 13, 1981, he rode through St. Peter's Square in an open car, nicknamed the "Popemobile." His bodyguards hated the car, but the pope insisted on being close to the people. That day, a gunman opened fire. Bullets struck the pope in the hand, shoulder, and stomach.

Fortunately the pope recovered from his injuries. And thirteen months later, he went to see Mehmet Ali Agca, the twenty-three-year-old Turkish terrorist who had tried to kill him. Sitting in the young man's prison cell, the pope forgave him. The awed prisoner asked, "Tell me why is it that I could not kill you?" The pope thought he knew the answer. He had a mission: to free the church in Communist lands.

The pope made a second trip to Poland in 1983 and a third trip in 1987. On each occasion, he gave his support to a

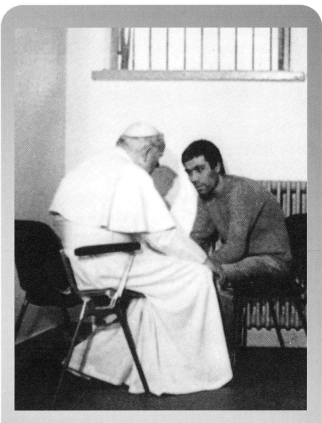

Pope John Paul II visits Mehmet Ali Agca, the terrorist who tried to kill him, in an Italian prison.

Polish workers' movement called Solidarity. Workers wanted the government to recognize their right to form a labor union to speak for them. Such a union, however, threatened Communist power. So the police filled the prisons with supporters of Solidarity.

The pope supported the workers' protests. In the speeches he made on his 1987 visit, he used the word "solidarity" hundreds of times. Each time he said "solidarity," his audience prayed, wept, cheered, and raised clenched fists. Solidarity now became more than a workers' movement—it was a fight for Polish freedom.

The timing was right. The Soviet Union had run out of money trying to impose communism on the world. Soon Poland and the rest of Eastern Europe shook off Communist rule. In 1991, the Soviet Union crumbled into separate nations. Later, Soviet president Mikhail Gorbachev would say, "Everything that happened in Eastern Europe these last few years would have been impossible without the presence of the pope and without the important role . . . that he played on the world stage."

HEALING OLD WOUNDS

The end of Soviet communism freed the pope of one wartime memory. But another one still haunted him—the horrible treatment of the Jews.

As pope, Wojtyla tried to bring Christians and Jews closer together. He was the first pope to set foot in a synagogue and listen to the story of the Jews retold. He went to Auschwitz, where so many Jews had died. He spoke to

Jewish leaders in every major city that he visited. He also made a historic decision in 1993—to recognize Israel as a nation. For nearly fifty years the church had not done so.

Pope John Paul II waves at the crowds from his Popemobile on a visit to Nazareth in the Holy Land.

The pope also worked to end hatred between Jews and Muslims and to end conflicts over control of the Holy Land, the lands around Jerusalem, the capital of Israel. All three religions—Islam, Christianity, and Judaism—consider the lands sacred. The pope dreamed of a time when members of these three great world religions—all believers in one God—could walk through the Holy Land in peace.

The actions and stands taken by the pope sometimes confused people. He worked hard to spread the Catholic religion. Yet he was more tolerant of the other religions than any pope in history. He disliked dictators. Yet he walked arm in arm with Fidel Castro, the Communist ruler of Cuba, to win greater freedom for Roman Catholics on the island. He believed in democracy. Yet he criticized the United States for caring more about selling its products to the world than selling peace.

BIRTHDAY CELEBRATION

In the year 2000, the pope turned eighty. By then he was one of the best-known people on the planet. A big birthday celebration was held in St. Peter's Square. That same year the Vatican put out a comic book based on the pope's life. There was only one problem. The pope hadn't finished his life's work.

In January 2001, the pope's doctor said, "I should order him to rest, but it would be useless." To prove him right, the pope set out on another round of world travels. One trip took him to Damascus, Syria. There he became the first pope to visit a mosque, the place where Muslims worship.

Though he struggled to walk and needed a cane, the pope was not yet ready to end his service to his church and the world's people. He had still other trips in mind.

IMPORTANT DATES

1920   Karol "Lolek" Wojtyla is born May 18 in Poland

1929   His mother Emilia dies

1932   His brother Edmund "Mundek" dies

1938   Graduates high school and begins college

1939   Nazis invade Poland; helps found underground theater

1940   Works in stone quarry

1941   His father Karol Sr. dies

1942   Trains as priest

1945   Soviet army takes control of Krakow; World War II ends

1946   Ordained as priest

1958   Appointed bishop of Krakow

1963   Appointed archbishop of Krakow

1967   Becomes one of two Polish cardinals

1978   Elected pope

1979   Makes first trip to Poland as pope

1981   Wounded by Turkish terrorist

1991   Soviet Union breaks apart

1993   Recognizes the nation of Israel

2000   Eightieth birthday celebration in Rome

INDEX

ABOUT THE AUTHOR

Deborah A. Parks—mountaineer, world traveler, and children's author and editor—brings a sense of adventure to all that she writes. She has written several highly acclaimed biographies, a book on mountaineering, and numerous magazine and newspaper articles for children and young adults. She has also been a contributor on many major educational projects. Her specialties are history, current events, and science. *John Paul II* is Parks's first work for The Millbrook Press. Parks lives in Fishkill, New York.